Harmony Close,

Kewtown,

Providenciales

Turks & Caicos Islands

ISBN: 978-1-0687399-0-3

BREAKING

THE BARRIERS

OF RELIGION

Table of Contents

CHAPTER 1

INTRODUCTION

Matthew 23:13-14

13 But woe unto you, scribes and Pharisees, hypocrites! for ye shut up the kingdom of heaven against men: for ye neither go in yourselves, neither suffer ye them that are entering to go in.

14 Woe unto you, scribes and Pharisees, hypocrites! for ye devour widows' houses, and for a pretence make long prayer: therefore ye shall receive the greater damnation.

Many today are still confused, living in denial, pretending to be what they are not, and cannot identify the truth because of them being religious. If you are someone who is constantly seeking the approval of your pastor or church assistant, wanting to be praised and seen for all your good works, you may be the right candidate that the enemy is using to carry out its many deceptive works of religion. If you are truly going to overcome this religious spirit, you must first be able to identify it, since religious spirits can manifest themselves in multiple ways. It is important to understand the different ways it can affect different people. For example, one person may experience the act of self-righteousness as a plague, while another person may be plagued with religious pride. So, we need to understand that the religious spirit affects many people in different ways.

CHAPTER 2

DEFINITION OF A RELIGIOUS SPIRIT

A religious spirit to the best of my knowledge is an outward act of falsehood, deceiving ourselves and others that we have it together by pretending to be spiritual through good deeds by living up to certain standards, a particular dress code, keeping or living up with certain doctrines and belief systems; having a form of Godliness but denying the power of God by refusing to become completely sold out to him by living a lifestyle of holiness according to the Word of God.

CHAPTER 3

SALVATION BY FAITH

Ephesians 2:8-10

8 For by grace are ye saved through faith; and that not of yourselves: it is the gift of God:

9 Not of works, lest any man should boast.

10 For we are his workmanship, created in Christ Jesus unto good works, which God hath before ordained that we should walk in them.

The scripture makes it very clear that salvation comes by grace through faith; it is not of oneself; it is God's gift to mankind, yet many become men-pleasers and not God chasers, believing that pursuing after men and being submissive make them in right standing with God. Many like their works to be seen and praised by men. They believe that such good works qualify them to be in good standing with God and men. Friends, we must never believe these fables. God doesn't want us to be naïve about this. He wants us to become liberated and set free from such deceptive acts and begin to pursue after Him with all our hearts. If we ought to become liberated from such strongholds, our devotion to God must be sincere.

Philippians 2:5-8

5 Let this mind be in you, which was also in Christ Jesus:

6 Who, being in the form of God, thought it not robbery to be equal with God:

7 But made himself of no reputation, and took upon him the form of a servant, and was made in the likeness of men:

8 And being found in fashion as a man, he humbled himself, and became obedient unto death, even the death of the cross.

CHAPTER 4

CALLED TO BE A GOD-CHASER

Friends, we must never allow the stronghold of the enemy to bind us by imprisoning our minds. If our minds are not aligned with the mind of God, we can never break free from such a stronghold. Our minds must be fully in God so that we can break these strongholds. Only then can we become God-chasers instead of men-pleasers. The scripture makes it very clear here that God desires that we, as His children, are not robbed of such blessings. We should display the character of a meek and humble servant being obedient and grateful for the finished work that God himself did for us on the cross, taking upon himself servanthood. This true act of love should play out in the lives of all true believers. We must be able to break free from all religious barriers by reprogramming our minds. Our minds are the battlegrounds. The victory is either won or lost here. If we are going to be a God-chaser, we must be able to shift our minds towards the things that will bring God glory and not ourselves. When we allow ourselves to take the glory and praise that belong to God, we are not being God chasers, but become self-promoters. It is at this pace that strong religious spirits are born. Self-promoting spirits are very strong religious spirits. These become manifestations of the flesh.

CHAPTER 5

THE WORKS OF THE FLESH

Galatians 5:19-26

19 Now the works of the flesh are manifest, which are these; Adultery, fornication, uncleanness, lasciviousness,

20 Idolatry, witchcraft, hatred, variance, emulations, wrath, strife, seditions, heresies,

21 Envyings, murders, drunkenness, revellings, and such like: of the which I tell you before, as I have also told you in time past, that they which do such things shall not inherit the kingdom of God.

22 But the fruit of the Spirit is love, joy, peace, longsuffering, gentleness, goodness, faith,

23 Meekness, temperance: against such there is no law.

24 And they that are Christ's have crucified the flesh with the affections and lusts.

25 If we live in the Spirit, let us also walk in the Spirit.

26 Let us not be desirous of vain glory, provoking one another, envying one another.

Our minds are the battleground. We must never think for a second that one can never go from self-promoting to the many works of the flesh. When our minds are not in the mind of God, it makes it easy for the enemy to take control of them. Our minds are the battleground, the victory is either won or lost in them. We must strive to become victorious there and must be able to shift our minds toward the things that will bring the glory of God. When such strongholds of religion have been broken, we no longer have to pretend to be someone we are not, but can now exercise true authority in Christ. We don't have to demonstrate falsehood but can live in the fulness of God's blessings, for the scripture makes it clear, that to be carnally minded is death, but to be spiritually minded is life and peace.

Romans 8:6-8

6 For to be carnally minded is death; but to be spiritually minded is life and peace.

7 Because the carnal mind is enmity against God: for it is not subject to the law of God, neither indeed can be.

8 So then they that are in the flesh cannot please God.

CHAPTER 6

OUR WORSHIP MUST BE AUTHENTIC

We must be willing to accept all that God has for us. When our minds are not in the right standing with God, the enemy uses them to his demise and advantage, he simply makes fools out of us, making us believe that we are in right standing with God, when in truth we are only being preyed upon. Our act of self - self-righteousness can be seen and, sure enough, the enemy is very much aware when our loyalty to God is not authentic. But when we put on the mind of Christ, we no longer serve as self-promoters but as God-chasers and our visions become clear.

Philippians 2:5

5 Let this mind be in you, which was also in Christ Jesus:

CHAPTER 7

PUTTING ON THE MIND OF GOD

Friends, so many battles have been lost simply because we have refused to put on the mind of Christ. If we ought to become overcomers of these religious spirits, we must be of a strong mind. Our minds must be in God's mind, rooted, grounded, and established. When we become strong roots in the mind of God, the enemy knows that he is in trouble, just as religion kills and binds, so we must become rooted in the truth of God's word, so that we can be able to break free from any religious spirit that kept us in prison for such a long time. We must understand that such spirits cannot be broken without the power of the Holy Spirit, so we must become spirit-filled by putting on the full armour of God.

Ephesians 6:11-17

11 Put on the whole armour of God, that ye may be able to stand against the wiles of the devil.

12 For we wrestle not against flesh and blood, but against principalities, against powers, against the rulers of the darkness of this world, against spiritual wickedness in high places.

13 Wherefore take unto you the whole armour of God, that ye may be able to withstand in the evil day, and having done all, to stand.

14 Stand therefore, having your loins girt about with truth, and having on the breastplate of righteousness;

15 And your feet shod with the preparation of the gospel of peace;

16 Above all, taking the shield of faith, wherewith ye shall be able to quench all the fiery darts of the wicked.

17 And take the helmet of salvation, and the sword of the Spirit, which is the word of God:

CHAPTER 8

THE ARMOUR OF GOD

Friends, it is never an easy task dealing with the spirit of religion, especially when so many are set in their different ways. Many of us may have been living a certain lifestyle or being men-pleasers, doing things our way for a long time until we become comfortable, and it seems right to us. Again, the scripture makes it clear, "There is a way which seemeth right unto a man, but the end thereof are the ways of death."

Proverbs 14:12

12 There is a way which seemeth right unto a man, but the end thereof are the ways of death.

Friends, the enemy wants us to stay in our current situations so that we don't become a God-chaser, but if we are going to break free from these religious barriers, we must be prepared to fight back by any means. We must never think for a second that these religious spirits are just mere things. To just write or talk about them is not an easy task. They are strong principalities that the enemy has been using for many decades to paralyse and cripple the true church of God from coming forth. You should be of a good understanding that it is not a building or some institution here that I am referring to but that of the real church which is you and me. The enemy knows that if the real church breaks through from such strongholds or if their eyes are no longer blinded, he knows that he is in trouble. Many great men and women of God have been bound by strongholds, serving in man-made tabernacles, refusing to be completely sold out to God by experiencing authentic worship and loyalty to Him. They believe that by being men-pleasers their good works put them in some high ranks in society and are unaware of how much they are in bondage by some man-made law and doctrine. A multitude of so-called secret societies have caused many people to be left crippled along their journey through life. Many had lost their lives and had never come to the knowledge of the truth. Today, I am encouraging many to break free from this stronghold and to become liberated from this darkness. God has called us to pursue after him, for in God there is no darkness. If we ought to kill these religious enemies, we must first be willing to get up and fight back. We must understand that our fight is not with each other. The enemy knows that if he can keep the real church, namely you and me, at war with each other, it makes his job easier. But we must be able to recognize what the enemy is doing and begin to rise up and take a stand. He is very much aware when your worship is not loyal to God, and it becomes a good place for him to take a high seat. You and I cannot afford to sit and be quiet about this. We must recognize what he is doing and begin to expose the many plots that he has been using for many centuries. When we begin to expose his plans, strongholds are broken and the many religious strongholds will come to naught, but to do so, we must rise and take that stand by putting on the armour of God.

Ephesians 6:17

17 And take the helmet of salvation, and the sword of the Spirit, which is the word of God:

CHAPTER 9

RELIGIOUS STRONGHOLDS

Please note that these religious spirits are strongholds that sit in many high places and have become strong principalities that have become invisible to the eyes by their deadly demonic spirits that had become rebellious and stubborn. No wonder why our fights have gotten harder because of the many different influences that come behind them. We must be able to discern with much understanding if we ought to war against such strongholds. These spirits are not easy to deal with, especially if you are not aware of them. For example, I recall times dealing with different individuals who had very strong, controlling spirits, but it was not just the spirit of control, I had noticed that on top of that these individuals were never wrong and there was always an answer that justified their wrongdoing. Even though I tried to express myself, it was almost to no avail, this spirit was high and speaking with so much authority to justify its wrongdoing that by the time it was finished with you, it would make you forget what you were expressing. I had experiences where these spirits would only smile when given a compliment; being around someone who is constantly mad or upset for no reason is not a good feeling at all and many times if you're in the company of these types of individuals or people

15

it will make you examine yourself, as if you had upset them, but friends this has nothing to do with you. These individuals who have these religious spirits are never happy, they don't have the joy of the Lord, and they are empty. Why? Because the void they have inside has never been filled up by the Holy Spirit. Their satisfaction comes from being a men-pleaser. When this happens, there is no real peace and joy on the inside. Many of you like me may have been around them, or maybe you could be living with such individuals who have these attributes, and you have been doing all you can to please these individuals by making them happy. Can I tell you that you are wasting your time, and it is time to deal with the spirit of religion. Please note that one or two signs do not determine if an individual has religious spirits, but you can tell by the multiple spirits that work up in these individuals daily, for example, no matter what you do or say these individuals are at most times depressed, never smiling and always opposing, most especially when you are helping them to come out of their current situations. Many of them will read the words of God, but there is no change. They have a form of Godliness but with no sincerity, it's their way or no way always telling you what to do and how to do it but when it comes to them, they are never admitting the truth. Here they are very self-centred and very quick to judge. Friends, we must never become afraid of such individuals when we identify that these individuals are bound, we must take the next step by overcoming such strongholds.

CHAPTER 10

BREAKING THE BARRIERS OF RELIGION

Friends, you and I have been anointed to win, we can never allow our lights to go out by allowing these religious spirits to suppress us to the place where we become drained. I am addressing this because many times I did not realize in the beginning that these spirits survive on the energy of others, for example where there is no talebearer the strike ceases.

Proverbs 26:20-21

Where no wood is, there the fire goeth out: So where there is no talebearer, the strife ceaseth. As coals are to burning coals, and wood to fire; So is a contentious man to kindle strife.

If you and I are to become skilled fighters, we must know our weapons, no good soldier is unaware of his many weapons. Let us have a look at the above scripture and quote, "Where there is no wood, the fire goeth out." To keep the fire burning, we must apply wood. If there is no wood there is no fire, likewise, we must use the silent treatment to come up against this religious spirit. Especially if we ought to protect our energies, religious spirits are strong spirits that just don't sit quietly, they seek prey that likes to argue or debate, be it the Word of God or some other carnality, they find delight in having the last words. Friends, we must be wise by protecting our energy from such strongholds. We must be always aware of the enemy's snare by using our weapon of silence, this does not mean we cannot speak, but we must know when to and when not to. If we ought to weaken this spirit and preserve our energies, our first step to overcoming is to use our weapons of silence; when we understand this weapon, not only will it save us our energies, but it will help us to identify the weakness that the spirit possesses.

Friends, I know what you are thinking, when I was unaware of what the religious spirit had been doing to me, I was always restless and fatigued, but after years of torment, I realised that this spirit was going nowhere and the enemy was using it to keep me in a stagnated place. Little did I know that the Holy Spirit was permitting it so that many could be set free from this stronghold. Many times in my walk with God, I thought I could have just bound this spirit and rebuked it. If you are like me, you may have thought the same thing. Please note that some of us may have had different experiences, but this becomes more severe when living with such individuals, be it a spouse or some other close relative. It is very important to know that when in close connection, your fight becomes even harder. Friends you can never bind or rebuke this spirit you must understand that these strongholds must be dealt with in a much different manner, by weakening this stronghold and suffocating it helps to keep it at bay or until it no longer affects you. This can only be done by recognizing the different ways you have been impacted by such spirits, for example, if you are only dealing with a self-righteous spirit then you must be able to strangle your victim by speaking the truth of God's Word but not overexerting yourself after speaking the truth of the Word. You must not allow the enemy to drain you, you must know how far to go by killing that prey with the silent treatment. There are multiple examples in the Word of God about these spirits. Here is a very good text in **Matthew 23:13-33**:

13 But woe unto you, scribes and Pharisees, hypocrites! for ye shut up the kingdom of heaven against men: for ye neither go in yourselves, neither suffer ye them that are entering to go in.

14 Woe unto you, scribes and Pharisees, hypocrites! for ye devour widows' houses, and for a pretence make long prayer: therefore ye shall receive the greater damnation.

15 Woe unto you, scribes and Pharisees, hypocrites! for ye compass sea and land to make one proselyte, and when he is made, ye make him twofold more the child of hell than yourselves.

16 Woe unto you, ye blind guides, which say, Whosoever shall swear by the temple, it is nothing; but whosoever shall swear by the gold of the temple, he is a debtor!

17 Ye fools and blind: for whether is greater, the gold, or the temple that sanctifieth the gold?

18 And, Whosoever shall swear by the altar, it is nothing; but whosoever sweareth by the gift that is upon it, he is guilty.

19 Ye fools and blind: for whether is greater, the gift, or the altar that sanctifieth the gift?

20 Whoso therefore shall swear by the altar, sweareth by it, and by all things thereon.

21 And whoso shall swear by the temple, sweareth by it, and by him that dwelleth therein.

22 And he that shall swear by heaven, sweareth by the throne of God, and by him that sitteth thereon.

23 Woe unto you, scribes and Pharisees, hypocrites! for ye pay tithe of mint and anise and cummin, and have omitted the weightier matters of the law, judgment, mercy, and faith: these ought ye to have done, and not to leave the other undone.

24 Ye blind guides, which strain at a gnat, and swallow a camel.

25 Woe unto you, scribes and Pharisees, hypocrites! for ye make clean the outside of the cup and of the platter, but within they are full of extortion and excess.

26 Thou blind Pharisee, cleanse first that which is within the cup and platter, that the outside of them may be clean also.

27 Woe unto you, scribes and Pharisees, hypocrites! for ye are like unto whited sepulchres, which indeed appear beautiful outward, but are within full of dead men's bones, and of all uncleanness.

28 Even so ye also outwardly appear righteous unto men, but within ye are full of hypocrisy and iniquity.

29 Woe unto you, scribes and Pharisees, hypocrites! because ye build the tombs of the prophets, and garnish the sepulchres of the righteous,

30 And say, If we had been in the days of our fathers, we would not have been partakers with them in the blood of the prophets.

31 Wherefore ye be witnesses unto yourselves, that ye are the children of them which killed the prophets.

32 Fill ye up then the measure of your fathers.

33 Ye serpents, ye generation of vipers, how can ye escape the damnation of hell?

Here, Jesus is dealing with the Pharisees. In this text, we can see multiple religious spirits, especially those of the self-righteousness ones. There are many others here, but we can never allow these spirits to wear us out and cheat us out of the many blessings that God has in store for us. We must be able to identify each one and apply our weapons in the areas that we need to use them. For example, here in **Matthew 12:1-2,** we see where Jesus went through the corn field on the Sabbath and his disciples began to pluck some heads of grain and eat them.

At that time Jesus went on the sabbath day through the corn; and his disciples were an hungred, and began to pluck the ears of corn and to eat.

2 But when the Pharisees saw it, they said unto him, Behold, thy disciples do that which is not lawful to do upon the sabbath day.

When the Pharisees saw this, they said to him that what his disciples were doing was unlawful to do on the Sabbath. Here is the judging spirit of these Pharisees, but what they fail to understand is that Jesus was Lord of the Sabbath. Here they had no reasoning, they were strong, argumentative teachers of the law, finding means and opposing ways to always justify their selfish actions. Jesus didn't go into any long argument with them, he went to the point and soon departed from them. Likewise, we must understand when to give man an answer and to use our weapons wisely so we cannot become drained by their many empty words.

CHAPTER 11

UNDERSTAND WHO YOU ARE

When you understand who you are and what you have been called to, it becomes less stressful when dealing with these spirits. The strong point I want you to see is that you are never to allow these spirits to drain you. You must be able to weaken them the majority of the time by ignoring their many empty words, using your most powerful weapon, that of silence. I know your eyes are now becoming open, and you will no longer be beaten up by this stronghold.

CHAPTER 12

YOU MUST WIN

After identifying such strongholds, one must be able to know the struggles one encountered in one's life; if you should by any means recognize that you have picked up the religious spirit, it is time to get rid of it once and for all. You must admit that not only did you suffer multiple delays but had wounded many soldiers along your life path and must come to the realization that it is time to free yourself and others from this place once and for all. Let us first examine the struggling area and begin to free ourselves from it. I must admit, it won't be easy in the beginning, but it will work in the end. There are many examples of self-righteous spirits that were carried out by different individuals in the Bible. Let us look at the Apostle Paul who was persecuting the church and killing the Christians. His self-righteous acts had led him to a place where God had to strike him down.

Acts 9:5-9

5 And he said, Who art thou, Lord? And the Lord said, I am Jesus whom thou persecutest: it is hard for thee to kick against the pricks.

6 And he trembling and astonished said, Lord, what wilt thou have me to do? And the Lord said unto him, Arise, and go into the city, and it shall be told thee what thou must do.

7 And the men which journeyed with him stood speechless, hearing a voice, but seeing no man.

8 And Saul arose from the earth; and when his eyes were opened, he saw no man: but they led him by the hand, and brought him into Damascus.

9 And he was three days without sight, and neither did eat nor drink.

But at the end of the assignment, the blind was lifted and his spiritual and physical sight were restored. God wants to restore us to our rightful positions. His never-failing love towards us is authentic. We don't have to question it at all. God wants a sincere heart that is turned towards Him.

Here is another familiar story of self-righteousness and greed that is found in **1Kings 21:1-13.**

And it came to pass after these things, that Naboth the Jezreelite had a vineyard, which was in Jezreel, hard by the palace of Ahab king of Samaria.

2 And Ahab spake unto Naboth, saying, Give me thy vineyard, that I may have it for a garden of herbs, because it is near unto my house: and I will give thee for it a better vineyard than it; or, if it seem good to thee, I will give thee the worth of it in money.

3 And Naboth said to Ahab, The LORD forbid it me, that I should give the inheritance of my fathers unto thee.

4 And Ahab came into his house heavy and displeased because of the word which Naboth the Jezreelite had spoken to him: for he had said, I will not give thee the inheritance of my fathers. And he laid him down upon his bed, and turned away his face, and would eat no bread.

5 But Jezebel his wife came to him, and said unto him, Why is thy spirit so sad, that thou eatest no bread?

6 And he said unto her, Because I spake unto Naboth the Jezreelite, and said unto him, Give me thy vineyard for money; or else, if it please thee, I will give thee another vineyard for it: and he answered, I will not give thee my vineyard.

7 And Jezebel his wife said unto him, Dost thou now govern the kingdom of Israel? arise, and eat bread, and let thine heart be merry: I will give thee the vineyard of Naboth the Jezreelite.

8 So she wrote letters in Ahab's name, and sealed them with his seal, and sent the letters unto the elders and to the nobles that were in his city, dwelling with Naboth.

9 And she wrote in the letters, saying, Proclaim a fast, and set Naboth on high among the people:

10 And set two men, sons of Belial, before him, to bear witness against him, saying, Thou didst blaspheme God and the king. And then carry him out, and stone him, that he may die.

11 And the men of his city, even the elders and the nobles who were the inhabitants in his city, did as Jezebel had sent unto them, and as it was written in the letters which she had sent unto them.

12 They proclaimed a fast, and set Naboth on high among the people.

13 And there came in two men, children of Belial, and sat before him: and the men of Belial witnessed against him, even against Naboth, in the presence of the people, saying, Naboth did blaspheme God and the king. Then they carried him forth out of the city, and stoned him with stones, that he died.

After Naboth refused to give Ahab his vineyard, his wife Jezebel had Naboth killed by sending letters signed by her husband

Ahab to the elders and nobles speaking falsely against an innocent man, just so her husband could have that which was not his. Here it is amazing to see what these spirits are capable of when we are not fully sold out to God. There is no telling the breadth and length one would go to and the mistakes one would make. There are more similar stories in the Bible, but I chose to make mention of these two so that you can understand that the works of the flesh can lead us into much trouble if we are not fully sold out to God. The enemy uses us as said earlier as prey to be preyed upon. If we are going to win over these destructive powers and break the many barriers of these religious spirits, we must be willing to rise and take a stand by identifying them and must be willing to fight back. I am more than convinced that your eyes are becoming open, and you are willing to take that stand in becoming all that God has called you to be.

CHAPTER 13

NAVIGATING THE STORM OF LIFE

We must never think for a second that we cannot beat the odds. I remember dealing with a very close individual who had multiple religious spirits. It seemed to me that they had them all, one in itself can become so frustrating, so imagine multiple. I had no idea how much I had been affected by them, I was mentally, physically, and emotionally exhausted. I was becoming so frustrated, I wanted to give in and quit. Furthermore, I remember several times before realizing the severity of these spirits, I wanted to give up completely. You must know when your eyes are not open to see what is happening to you, you're in a handicap position to fight. I was now becoming weak and fatigued. One must understand when you don't understand your wrestle you're a candidate for the enemy to prey upon. it wouldn't be so bad if you were dealing with one or two of these spirits when you go to church, but to be living and having to deal with it daily becomes nerve-wrecking, and I soon discovered that I was keeping sick and drained most of the time. It will amaze you when you understand that what you perhaps may have been going through was a result of these multiple spirits that you do not have much knowledge of -the enemy is happy when our eyes are not open. It is in these moments that he gets the best of us. Friends, I was quickly losing the battle. My physical strength was failing.

CHAPTER 14

NO PRAYER NO POWER

1Thesssalonians 5:17-18

Pray without ceasing. In everything give thanks: for this is the will of God in Christ Jesus concerning you.

One must realize when you have encountered these multiple religious spirits that are constantly draining your energy, it won't be long before your prayer life becomes ineffective. I had to figure this out. I am addressing this because it is very important to know that many of these demonic strongholds of religion blind you when you are unaware of what they are doing to you. You don't know what had been keeping you away from prayer life. Can I tell you, that if you are constantly fatigued by dealing with these spirits, you strengthen them and weaken yourself? By the time they are finished working on you physically, emotionally, and spiritually, they have drained most all the life out of you and left you weak and wrecked.

Matthew 12-43-45

43 When the unclean spirit is gone out of a man, he walketh through dry places, seeking rest, and findeth none.

44 Then he saith, I will return into my house from whence I came out; and when he is come, he findeth it empty, swept, and garnished.

45 Then goeth he, and taketh with himself seven other spirits more wicked than himself, and they enter in and dwell there: and the last state of that man is worse than the first. Even so shall it be also unto this wicked generation.

Now that your eyes are becoming open, you cannot afford to let the enemy continue his wicked demises. You must be willing to get up and fight back, I did it and so must you. Friends, we must never stay in such conditions. We must be able to navigate through these storms by getting out and fighting back. We must never say never, it is our time to soar above our prey. Furthermore, we must never again become so drained and wrecked by these spirits that we become malfunctioning. It is time to weaken our prey, and this can only be done by the grace of God. when we decide that we will no longer become a slave to fear, we are children of the most high God. When my eyes started to become open, the first thing God helped me to see was that I needed to be fully clothed by putting on my full armour. Let us go back here to **Ephesians 6:11-17**.

11 Put on the whole armour of God, that ye may be able to stand against the wiles of the devil.

12 For we wrestle not against flesh and blood, but against principalities, against powers, against the rulers of the darkness of this world, against spiritual wickedness in high places.

13 Wherefore take unto you the whole armour of God, that ye may be able to withstand in the evil day, and having done all, to stand.

14 Stand therefore, having your loins girt about with truth, and having on the breastplate of righteousness;

15 And your feet shod with the preparation of the gospel of peace;

16 Above all, taking the shield of faith, wherewith ye shall be able to quench all the fiery darts of the wicked.

17 And take the helmet of salvation, and the sword of the Spirit, which is the word of God:

If we want to win over these many religious enemies, we must be fully clothed. The Apostle Paul lets us know to stand against the enemy's schemes, first, we must understand our wrestle and know that we are not fighting each other. It is so important to understand this, many of these individuals are bound, and they want to be free and are fighting each other. However, these individuals are never our wrestle. We are wrestling against principalities, (against powers/unseen forces, against the rulers of the darkness, authorities of demonic agents) of this world, against spiritual wickedness in high places; therefore it is very important to stand with truth and righteousness and above everything we must have a shield of never wavering faith so that hell and all its agents can tremble and fall.

When I recognized that I was strengthening the enemy by answering back, it was in this place that by giving him what he wanted the enemy was aware and laughing at me. We must never cast our pearls before swine. In other words, we must know when to use our weapons of silence, by doing this we in return weaken our preys.

Matthew 6:7

7 But when ye pray, use not vain repetitions, as the heathen do: for they think that they shall be heard for their much speaking.

No wonder, my friends, we were being defeated. We must have a strong faith in knowing who our God is, and when we begin to use the wisdom of God by keeping these strongholds at bay, we will soon realize that our strength has been restored to us. We are no longer losing the many battles when our spiritual eyes are open. The enemy can no longer trick us after so many years of being beaten up. I am now a trained soldier, and you can be too. We must rise and use the many weapons that God has placed in our hands, and know when and when not to use them. You have been anointed and chosen to win, despite the many odds that were a testing of your faith. I now understand how to use each weapon and am constantly using them. I am now wiser and stronger, there is no looking back. The enemy is forever in trouble. You, too, can beat the odds and rise to a bigger and better you by breaking the many strongholds, silencing the voices of this treacherous enemy using your most powerful weapons, of prayer and silence. When we become candidates of much prayer and know how to use our weapon of silence, the enemy is forever in trouble. We must be of good understanding that what no longer serves a purpose in our lives cannot function again, so as to break the barriers of religion.

ABOUT THE AUTHOR

Apostle Rosemary Duncanson is a unique and rare vessel to the body of Christ. Apostle Duncanson was born in the Turks and Caicos Islands; she is a mother, Pastor, and Teacher. Having proclaimed the Word of God for more than three decades, her yoke-breaking anointing has helped many across all spheres of life. Apostle Duncanson enjoys her outreach ministries and reaches out to as many as possible, calling darkness into light. After many years of pain, hurt, and disappointments, she is proving her ministries entirely and is determined that the enemy will not win. Her determination has given her recognition in every area of her life.

LETTERS TO GOD